HOW DID WE FIND OUT ABOUT
SOLAR POWER?

HOW DID WE FIND OUT . . . series
Each of the books in this series on the history of
science emphasizes the process of discovery.

How Did We Find Out . . . ?
Books by Isaac Asimov

HOW DID WE FIND OUT ABOUT

SOLAR POWER?

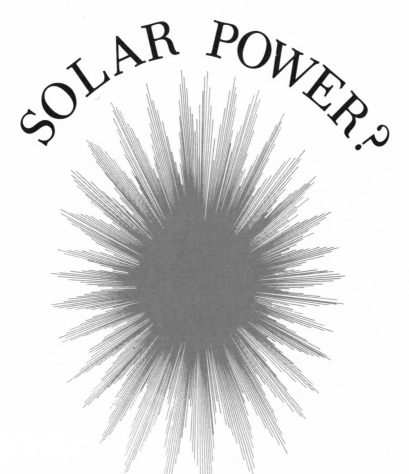

Isaac Asimov
Illustrated by David Wool

WALKER AND COMPANY
New York

Library of Congress Cataloging in Publication Data

Asimov, Isaac, 1920-
  How did we find out about solar power?

  (How did we find out—series)
  Summary: Describes the uses of the sun's energy
from the time of the Greeks and Romans to the
present day and discusses the potential of this
source of energy in our modern world.
    1. Solar energy—Juvenile literature.
2. Power resources—Juvenile literature.
[1. Solar energy. 2. Power resources] I. Wool,
David. II. Title.
TJ810.A78 1981   333.79'23   81-2469
ISBN 0-8027-6422-3   AACR2
ISBN 0-8027-6423-1 (lib. bdg.)

First published in the United States of America
in 1981 by the Walker Publishing Company, Inc.

Published simultaneously in Canada by Beaverbooks,
Limited, Don Mills, Ontario.

Printed in the United States of America

10 9 8 7 6 5 4 3 2 1

To
Nicholas Repanes
for lots of reasons

Contents

1 Sunlight

SOLAR POWER is the energy in sunlight and living things have always used it. Solar power is almost the only energy we have.

Green plants use the energy of sunlight to split water into the two substances that combine to make it up—hydrogen (HY-droh-jen) and oxygen (OK-sih-jen). They combine the hydrogen with carbon dioxide (KAHR-bon-dy-OK-side) from air and with minerals from water to make all the substances in the plant. This serves as food for animals—including us. It also makes all the wood we use.

The oxygen formed when the water is split moves out into the air. Animals breathe it to keep alive, and we do, too.

Green plants that lived many millions of years

ago were buried underground and turned into coal.* Tiny animal cells that lived in the sea on even tinier green plants were buried underground and turned into oil and natural gas.* Thus, the coal, oil, and gas we burn for energy came out of the sunlight of long, long ago.

Then, too, the warmth of sunlight heats the air, but it does so in an uneven way because different parts of the air get different amounts of sunlight at different times of the day and the year. This means there are masses of warm air and masses of cold air. The warm air is lighter than the cold air, so the warm air rises and the cold air moves in underneath. Because of sunlight we have winds, and we can get energy from the wind.

The sunlight also evaporates the ocean's water, which collects in the air as clouds. Under the right conditions, the droplets in the clouds combine to form larger drops that fall as rain. The rain pours off the land back into the ocean. From moving rivers and from waterfalls, we can get energy.

So you see, *almost all the energy we use traces back to the sun.*

None of this is what we mean when we talk of solar power these days, however. We mean the light and warmth of the sun, exactly as it reaches the earth. We don't mean the rain or the wind or coal or oil or even living plants. We mean just sunlight; the unchanged energy of the sun.

*See *How Did We Find Out About Coal?* (Walker, 1980)

*See *How Did We Find Out About Oil?* (Walker, 1980)

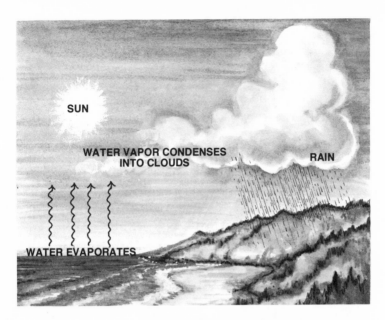

WATER CYCLE

There is a great deal of energy reaching the earth from the sun. Each year the total amount of energy reaching the earth in the form of sunlight is about 130 times as great as the energy contained in all the coal, oil and gas in the whole world.

What's more, the sun keeps on delivering that amount of energy to the earth each year, year after year after year. If scientists are right, the sun will keep doing this for 5 or 6 billion years.

To be sure, some of the sun's energy is used in heating the atmosphere and in producing winds and storms. Some is used to evaporate the ocean.

Some is absorbed by the plants. All of this takes up only a small portion of the sunlight, however. Most of the sunlight is absorbed by the earth itself.

The part of the sun's energy that is absorbed by the earth is not wasted, of course. It warms the earth. Without it, the earth would be very cold. Everything would freeze solid, and no life would be possible.

If the sun's energy kept being absorbed day after day, the earth's temperature would get higher and higher until everything melted and boiled and life would be destroyed. Fortunately, the earth gets rid of the energy it gains in the daytime by giving it off into space in the nighttime.

It is the balance between energy coming in by day and going out by night that keeps the temperature just right for the earth as a whole.

But suppose we used some of that energy from the sun. Would we be changing the balance and making trouble?

No. We wouldn't use up the energy. We can't use up energy. We can just change it from one kind to another, and it always ends up as heat. If we used some of the energy from the sun, that energy would still end up warming the earth— but we would get to use it first.

It would be like washing under a waterfall. We would lather up and then let the falling water rinse us off. After it had rinsed us it would still pour down into the river below. All the water

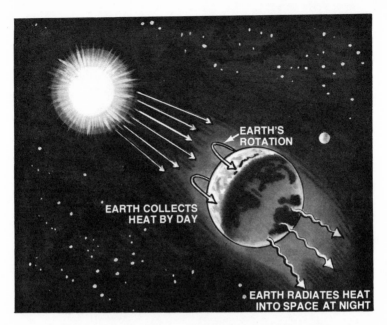

THE EARTH'S HEAT COMES FROM THE SUN

would still fill the river as before—but we would have used it first.

Of course, people *do* use the sun. On cool days we sit in the sunlight, and we walk on the sunny side of the street. That way we can get the warmth and feel more comfortable.

Houses built in cool areas were often built with openings facing south, even in ancient times, so as to have them catch the sunlight. In winter, when the sun is low in the sky and warmth is much more precious, the south side of the houses would catch the low shafts of sunlight particularly well.

• If a house is open to sunlight, it is also open to the cold wind, to rain, sleet, and snow. In the time of the Roman Empire, clear glass came to be used to cover the openings in the house. This let in sunlight but it kept out wind, dust, and bad weather.

• By closing the openings with glass, Romans

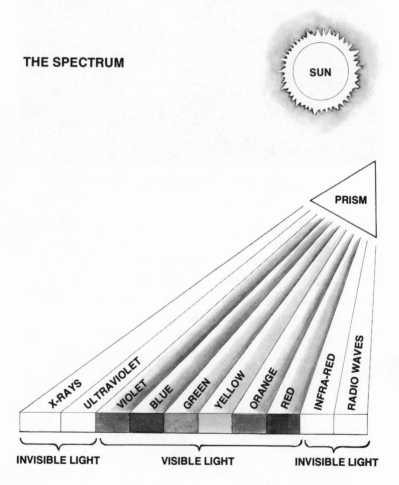

THE SPECTRUM

SUN

PRISM

X-RAYS · ULTRAVIOLET · VIOLET · BLUE · GREEN · YELLOW · ORANGE · RED · INFRA-RED · RADIO WAVES

INVISIBLE LIGHT — VISIBLE LIGHT — INVISIBLE LIGHT

who could afford it improved the warming of houses in the winter. The sunlight got in and warmed the air inside; the warm air couldn't get out again.

Warm air gives off heat in the form of infrared waves, which are something like light waves. The infrared waves are longer and don't affect our eyes, so we don't see them. Glass lets the short waves of the visible light waves from the sun pass inward into the house but doesn't let the longer infrared waves pass outward. This also helps keep the warmth inside the house.

Romans even built little houses of glass inside which plants could be grown. It might be too cold outside for them to grow but with the sun's warmth trapped inside, the plants did very well. These glass structures are called *greenhouses* because the plants make it green inside even when it is too cold for there to be much in the way of greenery outside.

The way in which glass (or some other substances) trap heat in this way is called *the greenhouse effect*.

After the Roman Empire fell, greenhouses were forgotten, but they were discovered again in modern times.

A GREENHOUSE

2 Mirrors and Hot Boxes

ARE THERE ways of concentrating the rays of the sun and squeezing them into a smaller area? More energy would then pour into that small area, meaning higher temperatures, and more use might be obtained from that energy.

• The ancient Greeks, and the ancient Chinese also, discovered that if light were reflected from a piece of polished metal that was *concave* (kon-KAVE; that is, that curved inward), the sun's rays would be concentrated. The sun's rays would come in *parallel* (PAR-uh-lel; that is, all heading in the same direction), but each ray would be reflected toward the center and all would come together.

The reflected rays would come together in a region called the *focus* (FOH-kus), a Latin word for "fireplace" because the temperature at that focus was so high it would set fire to things that burned easily.

• The first curved mirrors that were used for this purpose were in the shape of half-spheres. The rays were not reflected quite to a point. About 230 B.C., a Greek mathematician, Dositheus (doh-SITH-eeoos), showed that a mirror in the shape of a *paraboloid* (puh-RAB-uh-loyd) did better. A paraboloid is not shaped quite like a half-sphere, but is more like the small end half of an egg.

Sunlight reflected from the inner surface of a paraboloid would come together at the focus in a sharp point. The temperature at that point would be very high indeed.

Nowadays we know that if the paraboloid is curved perfectly and reflected all the light, the focus would be at a temperature equal to that of

**SMALL BURNING MIRROR
USED IN MIDDLE AGES**

the surface of the sun. The temperature would be 6,000° Celsius (10,000° Fahrenheit). It would be hot enough to burn anything that could burn, or to melt and boil anything that could not burn. Such mirrors are called *solar furnaces*.

* The ancient Greeks couldn't make such mirrors; no one could until recent times. Still, there is a story that the Greek mathematician Archimedes (AHR-kih-MEE-deez) built pretty good mirrors. When the Roman ships besieged his city of Syracuse on the coast of Sicily in 214 B.C., he is supposed to have used mirrors to reflect light toward the ships and set them on fire.

That particular story about Archimedes may not be true, but it shows that people later on thought about the possibility of using solar power in warfare.

* About A.D. 1000, an Arabian Moslem scientist, Alhazen (AL-hah-zen), living in Egypt, wrote a book about light and described paraboloid mirrors for concentrating it. About 1250, Roger Bacon, an English scholar who had read Alhazen's book, pointed out that such paraboloid mirrors might be used by Moslems as weapons against Christian armies. He suggested the Christians develop them first.

War mirrors were never built, though small ones were. They were used to melt small bits of metal. Large ones big enough to do damage at a great distance were simply too hard to build.

There were other ways to concentrate the heat of sunlight, however. After the Roman greenhouses were rediscovered, that notion was put to use.

ILLUSTRATION FROM ALHAZAN'S BOOK

A Swiss scientist, Horace de Saussure (soh-SOOR), designed glass boxes, one inside the other, in 1767. Each one trapped more heat than the one outside, and the innermost one would reach temperatures that were high enough to boil water.

Such *hot boxes* were sometimes used as novel-

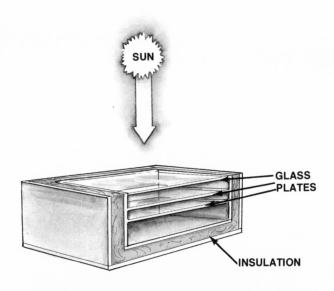

CROSS-SECTION OF DE SAUSSURE'S HOT BOX

ties. In the 1830s an English astronomer, John Herschel, was studying the stars from a place in South Africa. While he was there, he designed a hot box that he used for cooking a meal, using nothing more than sunlight.

Of course, making curved mirrors or hot boxes was a complicated job. It was much more convenient to burn wood or coal if one wanted heat with which to cook a meal or melt some metal, and that is what almost everyone did.

In 1769 a Scottish engineer, James Watt, built the first reasonably good steam engine. In this steam engine, the heat of burning wood or coal was used to boil water in a metal container. Steam formed and expanded. This expansion drove metal rods this way and that. The rods turned wheels and ran machinery.

SIR JOHN HERSCHEL

Such steam engines were quickly improved and made better and better. By 1800 there were about five hundred steam engines working in England. Little by little, they spread to the rest of Europe and to the United States.

They did all sorts of work that until then human and animal muscle had to do. They turned paddlewheels that made it possible for steamships to move against the wind and current. They turned wheels that moved steam locomotives over rails.

Steam engines started the *Industrial Revolution* and changed the way in which human beings lived.

In order for steam engines to work, wood or coal had to be burned constantly. There were places, though, where there wasn't much wood or coal in the vicinity. Wood and coal had to be brought in from distant points at considerable expense. Was there a more convenient way of forming steam?

Could energy from sunlight be used to boil water and produce the steam? In that way one could have a solar engine and the sunlight could be made to do work. This could be exciting, since sunlight was everywhere and it didn't cost anything.

Even in ancient times the sun had been used in this way. The Greek engineer Hero, in the time of the early Roman emperors, designed two containers that were connected to each other by a tube. There was water at the bottom of one and the connecting tube led from that bottom to the top of the second. If the container with the water was placed in the sun, the air inside would expand and force the water through the tube and into the upper container.

In that way, water was pushed upward and sunlight did the work. However, Hero's device was just a toy.

It was also possible for sunlight to expand air and force it through organ pipes so that it made a musical note. There were some ancient statues that made a musical note when the light of the rising sun struck them. Worshipers thought it was a miracle, but it was just expanding air.

• The first modern scientist to be interested in solar engines was a Frenchman named Augustin Mouchot (moo-SHOW). In 1861, he used hot boxes and made them even hotter by allowing sunlight to fall upon them after having been concentrated by a curved mirror.

He could use this device for pumping water as Hero did, but much more quickly and in greater quantities. He could use it for cooking food, as Herschel did, and for boiling alcohol out of wine.

It was not till 1866 that Mouchot built a hot box of this sort that was large enough to boil water quickly enough to run a steam engine.

The device was large and clumsy and besides, in France, the sun didn't shine all the time. In winter, especially, there were many cloudy days. Much of the time, therefore, Mouchot didn't have a chance to use his solar engine at all.

Mouchot therefore went on to the French colony of Algeria in North Africa. There was much

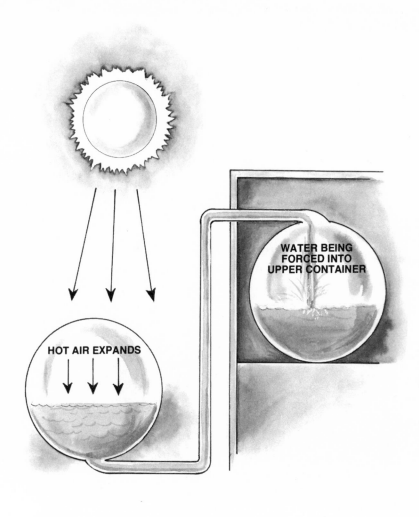

HERO'S DEVICE

more sunlight there. What's more, there was no coal there, so solar engines would be particularly useful. In North Africa he built many solar engines that were used for various purposes.

Although such solar engines worked, they were much more expensive than ordinary steam engines.

This may seem strange, considering that sunlight is free. However, there are parts of the engine that are not free at all. A curved mirror for concentrating sunlight is expensive and easily damaged. What's more, it had to be turned all the time so as to have it face the sun, and that was a troublesome job.

Is there some way of doing away with the need to concentrate sunlight? Could one make do with the lower temperature of ordinary sunlight that wasn't concentrated.

MOUCHOT'S SOLAR ENGINE, PARIS 1878

Lower temperatures would work if one used liquids that boiled at a lower temperature than water does. There is ammonia, for instance, which boils at $-33°$ Celsius ($-28°$ Fahrenheit). It is a gas to begin with, but if the gas is put under pressure, it will turn into a liquid. Then ordinary sunlight, by heating it just a little, will turn it back into a gas. The ammonia gas will expand and do the work of steam.

The first person to build such a low-temperature solar engine was a French engineer, Charles A. A. Tellier (tel-YAY). He also realized that it wouldn't work very well in the climate of France, and in 1890 he published a book describing how well such engines would work in Africa.

Similar low-temperature solar engines were built in the American southwestern desert areas in the early 1900s. The best and largest of the kind was built in Africa by an American engineer named Frank Shuman. Just as things looked hopeful for it in 1914, World War I came along and ruined his hopes. Shuman died before the war was over.

The real problem with solar engines, however, was that ordinary steam engines were still being improved and made better. What's more, new sources of fuel were found.

After World War I, oil began to be used more and more as fuel. It was far more convenient than coal and there seemed no point to try working with solar engines that were much more difficult to handle.

3 Hot Water

OF COURSE, water doesn't always have to be boiled to be useful. Sometimes merely warm water is sufficient. As an example, while it isn't at all comfortable to wash in cold water, it is even worse trying to wash in very hot water. Moderately hot water is best for washing. This is true not only for washing the body, but also for washing dishes and clothes if you have to do this with your hands.

Still, to get the water warm enough to use for washing still means heating it over a fire of some sort. Since considerable water must be used for washing, it usually has to be a big fire that is kept going for quite a while.

It's hard work splitting wood or dragging coal in to keep the fire going, and it can run into expense, too. For that reason, it was usual in the days before this century to have one particular day each week as "wash day" so that the hard work could all be concentrated into one day. What's more, people would take a hot bath only once a week.

But what if the sun did the work? A tank of water left in the sunshine would get warm, wouldn't it?

Yes, it would, but it would take a long time, at least half a day and, then, if it got cloudy, or especially if night came, the water would cool off quickly.

* In 1891, though, an American inventor named Clarence M. Kemp put cylinders of water inside a box that was lined with felt to make it harder for the heat to escape. The top of the box was made of glass. In this way you had a hot box.

Sunlight could get through the glass to heat up the water, and the heat couldn't easily get out through the felt. The inside warmed up more quickly and stayed warm longer. People began to put such solar water heaters on their roofs where they could be exposed to the sun. Pipes led the water into the house, and as the hot water was used, more cold water could enter the tanks to be warmed.

The water still cooled off fairly quickly at night through the glass, which was exposed to the cold night air, so there was never any warm water in the morning.

* In 1909 an American engineer, William J. Bailey, corrected that. He arranged to keep just a small amount of water in coiled pipes in the tank on the roof. This water heated up quickly because there wasn't much of it. It was then moved

CLARENCE M. KEMP

through other pipes into a storage tank in the kitchen. This storage tank was lined on all sides with materials that wouldn't let heat escape easily.

During the day more and more hot water was added to the kitchen storage tank. During the night no more was added, but what was already in the storage tank cooled off very slowly, and there was warm water for bathing and washing in the morning. As the morning wore on, more hot water began to be added.

Naturally, this sort of thing worked best in climates where there was a lot of sunshine and

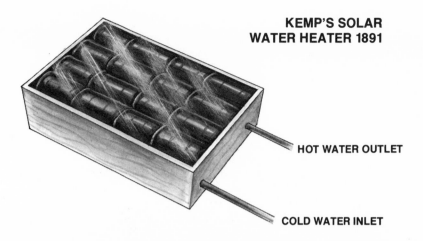

HOT WATER OUTLET

COLD WATER INLET

where the temperatures were quite warm. A lot of sunshine meant a lot of hot water, and warm temperatures helped keep the water from cooling off. It was for this reason that solar water heaters were particularly popular in places like southern California. The notion also spread in Arizona and New Mexico and later on in Florida.

Again, however, advances of other kinds made solar water heaters seem less desirable.

For instance, new supplies of natural gas were discovered. That meant that gas was more available and cheaper than it ever was. To heat up water, you no longer had to chop wood or lug coal. You simply had a water tank with a gas jet underneath. You turned on the jets and set fire to the gas and the water would heat up. It could be done at night, on cloudy days, in the winter—whenever hot water was needed.

In fact, the hot water tank could be outfitted with a *thermostat*. This is a device that reacts to changes in temperature. If the temperature in the

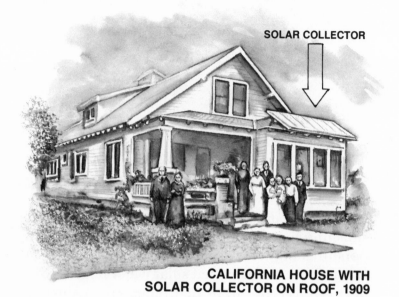

SOLAR COLLECTOR

**CALIFORNIA HOUSE WITH
SOLAR COLLECTOR ON ROOF, 1909**

water tank got low enough, the thermostat automatically shifted in such a way as to light the gas. When the temperature got high enough, the thermostat shifted again and shut the gas off. In this way, the water was always at the right temperature, never too cold and never too hot.

Later on, electric heaters came in that could keep the water hot without danger of gas explosions or gas leaks.

Then, too, as hot water became easier to get, people bought automatic dish washers and clothes washers and installed additional bathrooms and showers. In this way, they came to need more hot water than a solar water heater could supply.

After World War II, which ended in 1945, there

A SOLAR HOUSE IN DIAGRAM FORM

was the biggest boom in the use of oil and gas. During the war it had seemed important to save as much fuel as possible for use by the armed forces, but after the war people felt they could pamper themselves.

As it happened, great new oil fields were discovered in the Middle East, and suddenly there seemed to be more oil and gas than people could possibly use. Everywhere people could get all the heat they wanted from new oil furnaces without any trouble at all. No shoveling coal, no lugging out ashes. You just had someone fill an oil tank and a thermostat did all the work.

Oil was never so cheap as it was in the 1950s and 1960s, and no one seemed interested in solar power at all. It just didn't seem necessary.

4 Nuclear Power and Oil

THE NEW oil fields of the Middle East were not the only reason why the world felt no need for solar energy in the years after World War II.

Back in 1896, it was discovered that certain kinds of atoms, such as those of uranium (yoo-RAY-nee-um) and thorium (THAW-ree-um), the two most complicated atoms then known, gave off very tiny particles. These particles were much smaller than atoms, so they were called *subatomic particles*. This was known as *radioactivity*.

In the course of this process, each uranium or thorium atom gave off a surprising amount of heat. It was much more heat than was produced per atom when oil or coal or wood combined with the oxygen in the air and burned.

The heat of radioactivity was produced as the

result of changes that took place in the atomic *nucleus* (NYOO-klee-us), a tiny object at the very center of the atom. These changes produced what is therefore known as *nuclear energy.**

For years it didn't seem that nuclear energy was important because although there was a surprising amount of it for each atom, few atoms underwent the change at any one time. For that reason, much more *total* energy could be obtained out of a small wood fire than out of a lump of uranium.

In 1939, however, it was discovered, to the surprise of scientists, that unusual things happened

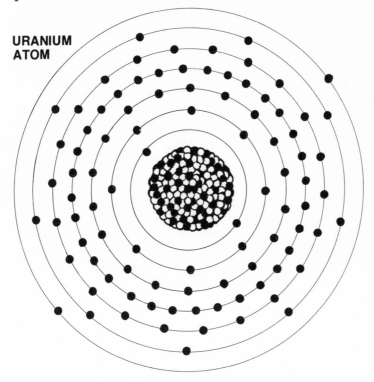

URANIUM ATOM

*See *How Did We Find Out About Nuclear Power?* (Walker, 1976)

to uranium atoms when they were struck by a kind of subatomic particle called a *neutron* (NOO-tron). When a uranium atom absorbs the neutron, it splits into nearly equal halves. This is called *uranium fission* (FISH-un).

Several neutrons are given off in the fission process. Each of those neutrons might strike another uranium atom and cause it to undergo fission, too, producing still more neutrons. This builds up rapidly and, in a tiny fraction of a second, trillions of uranium atoms are all undergoing fission.

A uranium atom that undergoes fission produces more energy than one that simply gives off a subatomic particle. If very large numbers of uranium atoms are undergoing fission, enormous energies are produced.

It is a particular and rather rare variety of uranium, one that is called *uranium 235*, that undergoes fission. During World War II, the United States learned how to concentrate uranium 235 and cause it to undergo a fission buildup. They kept the fissioning atoms tightly together for a fraction of a second, just long enough to let the energy increase to a large amount. After that fraction of a second, the energy built up to the point where there was the enormous explosion of a *nuclear bomb*. Such nuclear bombs were first exploded in 1945.

After World War II the United States (and other nations as well) learned how to allow uranium fission to take place in such a way that there was no explosion. The uranium atoms merely went on

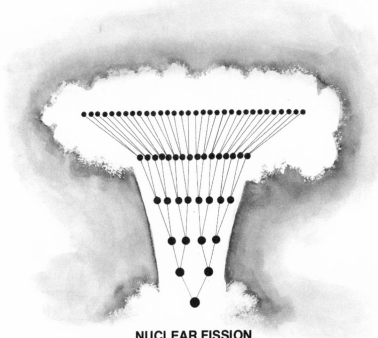

NUCLEAR FISSION

fissioning in an orderly way, producing a great deal of energy that could be used for a great many purposes.

In the 1950s and 1960s, nuclear power plants were built all over the world and many people felt that by the year 2000, uranium fission would be the major supplier of the world's energy.

But then things started to go wrong with both uranium and oil.

In the case of uranium fission there were radiation problems. Subatomic particles could be dangerous. So could X rays and gamma rays, which were also produced by the fissioning atoms. (These were like light waves but very much shorter and much more dangerous.)

To be sure, the dangers in fission could be guarded against and nuclear power plants have never killed anybody by radiation. Still, in order to make sure that the plants remain safe, they have to be built very carefully and with many safety devices. This makes nuclear power plants very expensive and it takes a long time to build them.

And even so, many people fear them and are against having them built at all.

Then, too, after the uranium atoms have split in two, what is left over are smaller atoms that are radioactive and continue to give off dangerous subatomic particles for many years. This *radioactive waste* must be buried somehow in such a way that none of it will ever get into the soil or rivers

THREE MILE ISLAND

or air. Some people aren't sure that this can be done safely as more and more of the radioactive waste is produced. They think the radioactivity might poison the world eventually.

As for oil, the most important difficulty there is that it is running out.

Most people didn't seem to be willing to think of this in the energy-happy days of the 1950s and 1960s, but actually there isn't much oil in the ground. A great deal of oil was being burned by the people of the world each year, and the quantity kept going up year by year. At the rate the oil was used, it seems likely that the oil isn't going to last for very long past the year 2000.

The United States, which had produced more oil than any other nation, but which also used more oil than any other nation, began to run short of oil after 1970. The amount of oil it produced reached a peak after which it produced less and less each year. As it continued to use more and more, it began to have to import oil from the Middle East.

That was not so bad for a while, but the Middle East was a troubled area. From 1920 on, it had been controlled chiefly by Great Britain and France, but after World War II the nations of the Middle East became independent. They took over their own oil wells, then banded together to raise the price.

Toward the end of 1973 there was a short boycott during which the Middle Eastern nations refused to ship oil to the United States and certain other countries. At once there were gasoline lines in the United States and Americans began to realize how much they depended on foreign countries for essential energy. What's more, after the boycott the price of oil increased rapidly, and it became expensive indeed.

The happy days of energy that was cheap and plentiful were over, and more and more people realized that oil would not last for more than a few decades. What next?

One way out would be to continue building nuclear power plants. More and more people are afraid of that, however, especially after one plant at Three Mile Island in Pennsylvania had a bad accident in 1979 (though no one was killed).

Another way out would be to make more use of coal, since there is still plenty of that. Coal, however, is difficult to mine and to carry from place to place. It pollutes the air when it is burned (so does oil, by the way). What's more, it forms the gas, carbon dioxide, when it burns (so does oil), and many scientists think that if the carbon dioxide in the air increases by even a small amount, it may change earth's climate and make it worse.

There are other sources of energy, such as the wind, water currents, tides, and the earth's heat deep underground. Each has its drawbacks, and all of them together might not be enough.

One possible source for the future is *nuclear fusion*. This is another kind of nuclear energy that doesn't involve uranium. It works by smashing small atoms of hydrogen together to form the slightly larger atoms of helium (HEE-lee-um.) It

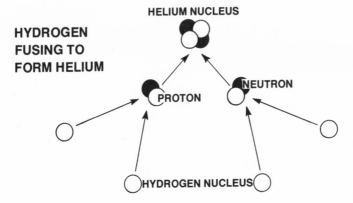

HYDROGEN FUSING TO FORM HELIUM

HELIUM NUCLEUS

PROTON

NEUTRON

HYDROGEN NUCLEUS

is this fusion energy that powers the very power-ful *hydrogen bombs*.

Fusion yields more energy and less radiation than fission does. Hydrogen is easier to get and to handle than uranium is, and there is enough hydrogen of the kind we need to last for billions of years.

The catch is that although we can use fusion in huge bombs, we can't control it to make it yield energy slowly and safely. We may learn how to do so soon, but up to now scientists have been working at the problem for thirty years and still haven't succeeded.

While we are waiting for nuclear fusion to be worked out, is there anything else?

Well, there is solar power. The sun is always shining, and there was considerable progress in learning how to use it before cheap oil came along. Might we return to it now?

If we use solar power to heat water and even houses, if we use it to run some machines, that would certainly cut down the quantity of fuel we would need to burn.

But perhaps we can do even more. Nowadays, people are using energy in the form of electricity for almost everything they do, because there is nothing that is quite so convenient in many ways as electricity.*

The way electricity is produced usually is by forcing wheels to turn between the poles of large magnets. The wheels can be made to turn by rapidly moving water, as at Niagara Falls. Mostly, though, they are made to turn by the force of steam produced by water that is heated by burning coal or oil.

Can solar energy be used to boil water and form steam that will turn the wheels to produce electricity?

Perhaps that is not necessary. There may be a better way.

STEAM TURBINE

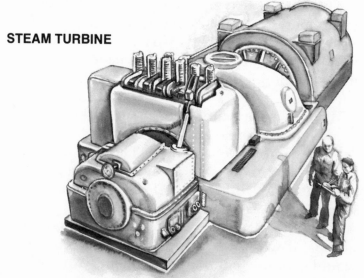

*See *How Did We Find Out About Electricity?* (Walker, 1973)

5 Solar Cells

OUTSIDE THE central nucleus of atoms are one or more tiny particles called *electrons*. It is when these electrons break loose and drift from one atom to another that an electric current is set up.

Sunlight has enough energy to cause the electrons of certain kinds of atoms to work loose. In that case, substances containing those atoms could produce an electric current if they were exposed to light.

Long before scientists knew anything at all about electrons, they discovered this connection of light and electricity. In 1873 a chemist, Willoughby Smith, discovered accidentally that the metal, selenium, could conduct an electric current when light shone on it. In the dark it did not conduct an electric current.

At first this was merely considered a curiosity, since the amount of electricity that was produced was tiny. Eventually, though, certain uses were found.

Selenium can be used, for instance, in so-called *electric eyes*. An electric eye is a small container from which all the air has been pumped out. It contains a metal surface covered with a layer of selenium. When light shines on it, electrons are given off by the selenium and the result is a small electric current flow. The flowing electric current may trigger a relay that allows a larger electric current to hold a door closed even though there is a spring acting to pull it open.

Suppose an electric eye is on one side of a hall, just in front of a door, and a tiny light on the other side of the hall shines on the electric eye. As long as the light shines, the door stays closed. If a person approaches the door, however, his body gets in the way of the light. The electric flow in the electric eye stops as the person passes and the door opens.

Such an electric eye is an example of a *photoelectric* (FOH-toh-ee-LEK-trik) cell where *photo* is from a Greek word for "light." If a photoelectric cell works when sunlight falls on it, it would be a *solar cell*.

For a long time, photoelectric devices were used only for such small items as magic eyes because they produced only tiny amounts of electricity. Selenium, for instance, turns less than 1 percent of the energy of the sunlight that falls upon it into electricity.

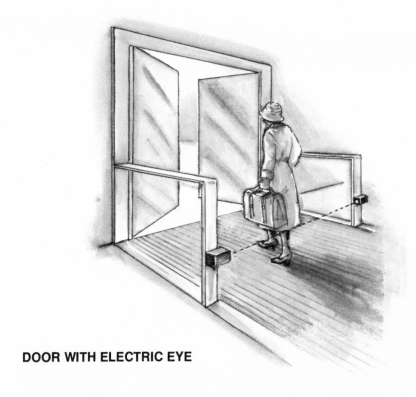

DOOR WITH ELECTRIC EYE

Meanwhile, scientists had long been working on the problem of controlling electric currents and making them change in strength and other ways very rapidly and delicately.

Through most of the century, glass bulbs with no air inside were used. These bulbs contained metal inserts, and electrons could be made to pass through the vacuum from one metal insert to another when one of the inserts was heated. By altering the properties of the inserts from the outside, the flow of electrons could be made to go faster or slower. By setting up very rapid changes in the flow of electrons in this way, radio, television, and other *electronic devices* were made possible. In fact, the glass bulbs are commonly called *radio tubes*.

In 1948 it was discovered that certain materials that ordinarily don't conduct electric currents could have electrons knocked out of their atoms. They would then conduct the currents fairly well, so they were called *semiconductors*.

If semiconductors were made of very pure substances with just a little of certain kinds of other atoms added, electrons could be made to come loose with particular ease and those electrons could be controlled. They could be made to go faster or slower just as in radio tubes. These semiconductor devices were called *transistors* and, little by little, transistors took the place of tubes.

Transistors didn't have to be heated as tubes had to be so that transistorized devices started without any "warm-up" period. Transistors were rugged, didn't break, didn't wear out. Most important of all was that transistors could be made much smaller than tubes.

Instruments that used transistors could be made much smaller than before. You could have pocket radios or pocket computers run on tiny batteries because transistors ran with much less electric current than tubes did.

By the 1950s many scientists were very much interested in transistors.

One of the materials out of which transistors

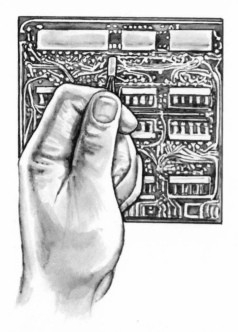

TRANSISTOR

could be made is *silicon* (SIL-ih-kon). This is a very common substance, the second most common on earth. The sand and rocks all about us are about one-quarter silicon.

In 1954, scientists at Bell Telephone Laboratories (where the transistor was invented) were working with silicon to try to make it do the job better. Quite by accident, they noticed that when silicon was exposed to light, an electric current appeared.

Silicon did much better than selenium did. About 4 percent of the energy of the sunlight that

SILICON SOLAR CELLS

BELL SOLAR BATTERY

fell upon the silicon was turned into electricity.
That was five times as efficient as selenium.

Scientists continued to work on the silicon,
adding tiny bits of other substances and finally
managed to produce samples of silicon that
turned 16 percent of the energy of sunlight into
electricity.

There was a catch, to be sure.

The silicon atoms that make up a quarter of all
the sand and rocks in the world are strongly at-
tached to oxygen atoms. Breaking that attachment
and getting out the silicon atoms by themselves is
a hard job, taking a lot of effort, time, and energy.

Silicon obtained in this way is quite expensive. Then, once you have a solid chunk of silicon, it must be shaved into very thin wafers and just the right amount of impurities must be added. More expense. Finally, a single silicon solar cell produces just a small amount of electricity, even if it is better at it than selenium is. To get enough electricity for most needs, there must be many solar cells all working together.

Silicon solar cells have proved their value in space however.

Beginning in 1957, the Soviet Union and the United States began to put artificial satellites into orbit about the earth. Eventually, they began sending probes out to the moon and to other planets, even as far away as Saturn, which is 800 million miles from earth.

The satellites and probes needed power to run the instruments they carried and the radios with which they stayed in contact with earth. The power supply had to be very light and it had to keep on working for anywhere up to years of time.

Solar cells seemed just the thing. The United States used them to power its satellites and they worked very well.

That, however, was because not much energy was needed for the satellites, and because there was no other power supply that would work nearly as well.

On earth itself it was a different matter. Solar cells couldn't compete. Electricity produced in other ways was much, much cheaper. Through the 1960s and even the 1970s, electricity from sunlight remained a dream.

SATELLITE WITH SOLAR COLLECTOR PADDLES

6 Deserts and Space

TIMES ARE changing in two ways as the 1980s begin.

In the first place, the price of oil keeps going up steadily, and other fuels will become more expensive too, as the need for them increases.

On the other hand, scientists will probably keep on learning ways to make better solar cells more cheaply. In twenty years, the amount of solar cell electricity you could buy for a dollar has increased about two hundred times. It is still hundreds of times too expensive to compete with electricity from burning fuel, but solar electricity may continue to get cheaper and fuel electricity will surely continue to get more expensive. Eventually, it may prove desirable to switch to solar cells.

Of course, although the energy in sunlight is great, it is thinly spread out. That is the big disadvantage of sunlight compared with fuel.

If you want a great deal of energy from fuel, you can pile a great deal of wood or coal or oil in one place. You can't do this with sunlight. You can't pile it up. You have to collect it over a large area.

You would have to place solar cells over thousands of square miles of land in order to produce enough electricity for the uses of the United

States. You would have to place them over tens of thousands of square miles to produce enough electricity for the use of the world.

Fortunately, there is enough land. There are millions of square miles of sunny desert land in the world, land that isn't used for very much. There is the Sahara Desert, which is as large as the United States. There are also large desert areas in Saudi Arabia, in Iran, in western Australia, in the southwestern United States and so on.

Still, it would take a lot of money, effort, and time to coat the necessary areas with solar cells. The areas would have to be protected from wild animals, from terrorists or vandals, from sandstorms and other natural accidents.

What's more, the surface of the earth has disadvantages as far as exposure to the sun is concerned. Certain conditions might obscure the sun. Sandstorms could not only damage the solar cells, but would cut off the sunlight. Clouds, mist, fog, smoke, all would cut off the sunlight and, therefore, reduce the output of electricity.

In hot desert areas, of course, there wouldn't be much in the way of clouds and so on, and perhaps sandstorms wouldn't be frequent. We might suppose that for the most part there would be clear skies and bright sunlight.

Even so, perfectly clear air absorbs a considerable amount of sunlight. When the sun is high in the sky, the absorption isn't much, but when it is lower in the sky, the sunlight must pass through a greater thickness of air to reach the ground and more is absorbed. Then, at night, of course, there is no sunlight at all.

Electricity would be produced mostly for a few hours around noon each day.

Can we do better?

Some people think so.

Suppose we set up a large area of solar cells in space right over some point on earth's equator. If such a *space solar power station* (SSPS) were placed about 22,000 miles high, it would move

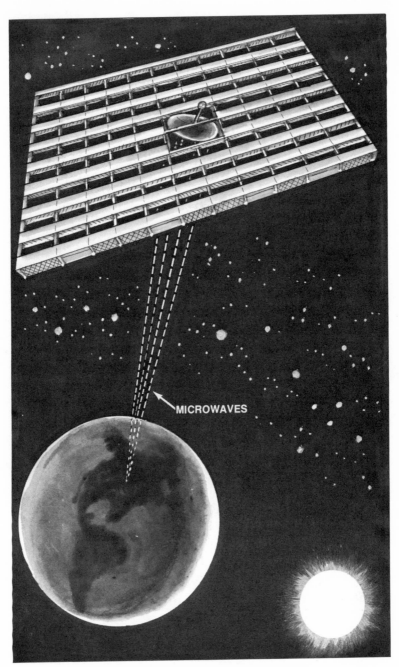

SPACE SOLAR POWER STATION

around the earth in twenty four hours. The earth turns on its axis in twenty four hours so that to someone who is directly under the SSPS it would seem to remain directly overhead at all times.

Such an SSPS would remain in sunshine at all times, for even when it moved to the opposite side of the earth from the sun, it would miss the earth's shadow because the earth's axis is tilted. It is only during the time around the two equinoxes (March 20 and September 23) that the SSPS would spend a few hours each night in the shadow. In the course of the year, the SSPS would be hidden from the sun only 2 percent of the time.

What's more, there is no atmosphere in space to absorb any of the sunlight at any time. Nor would there be any wildlife, or any vandals to damage the cells. About the only thing that could hurt them would be occasional small meteors and that would be a very rare thing.

On the whole, it may be that a number of solar cells could produce 60 times as much electricity in space over the course of a year as the same number could produce on earth.

Of course, producing electricity in space isn't going to do us any good here on earth, unless that energy could be brought down to us. One way of doing that would be to convert the electricity into *microwaves*, which are the kind of short-wave radio waves that are used in radar. These microwaves could be beamed down to earth and caught in special receivers which would convert it back to electricity. The microwaves could be concentrated into a tight beam so that the size of the receivers would be much less than those that would be needed to catch sunlight.

Some of the energy would be lost in converting electricity to microwaves and then back to electricity, but, in the end, a receiver of a given size could produce far more electricity from the microwaves than that same area of solar cells receiving sunlight.

Some people think that microwaves might be dangerous. However, the microwaves could be collected in places far from where many people live. It is also easy to arrange to have the microwave beam spread out thinly or stop altogether at any time, as, for instance, when an

MICROWAVE RECEIVER

airplane accidentally approaches it. The microwaves would certainly not be as dangerous as allowing the earth to run out of energy.

To be sure, we couldn't make do with a small number of solar cells. The area of solar cells in a single SSPS would have to be enormous. There might have to be several square miles of cells. Even so, a single SSPS would be far from enough to supply earth with all the energy it needs. There would have to be a chain of many dozens of them circling the earth high in the sky above the equator.

It would take hundreds of billions of dollars to put them up, but the people of earth are willing to spend hundreds of billions of dollars each year on various military machines that do nothing but consume energy in vast amounts. Perhaps if we could work out some way of bringing about peace on earth, we could spend some of the money we now waste on guns, tanks, ships, and planes to make sure we all have the energy we need.

This is not to say that we must depend on solar power only. By the time we have even the first SSPS in orbit, scientists may have worked out controlled nuclear fusion. We might be using winds, tides, and other energy sources in new and improved ways, too.

And if we can put all these energy sources into producing electricity, we can have everything else. For instance, we can never run out of fuel in that case. Electricity can be used to break water into hydrogen and oxygen.

WINDMILL ON BUILDING

Hydrogen is itself a very good fuel, and when it burns, it combines with oxygen and becomes water again. Nothing is used up but the electricity, which comes from the energy of sunlight, and that will last for billions of years.

Hydrogen is explosive, to be sure, and quite dangerous to use. There is no reason, though, why ways couldn't be worked out to combine the hydrogen with carbon dioxide from the air to form a gas called *methane*. This burns more safely than hydrogen does, and when it burns, it just produces the water and carbon dioxide out of which it was originally made.

It could be that if we have the courage and vision to use the sun—which is waiting there to be used—human beings will be far better off in time to come than they have ever been before.

Index